SEA OTTERS

Published by Creative Education, Inc., 123 South Broad Street, Mankato, Minnesota
56001

Library of Congress Cataloging-in-Publication Data

Brust, Beth Wagner.
Sea otters / by Beth Wagner Brust.
p.   cm. — (Zoobooks)
Summary: Describes the physical characteristics, habitat, life cycle, and daily activities
of this member of the weasel family.
ISBN 0-88682-415-X
1. Sea otter—Juvenile literature. [1. Sea otter.] I. Title. III. Series: Zoo books
(Minneapolis, Minn.)
QL737.C25B78   1991   599.74'447—dc20   91-9939 CIP AC

A OTTERS

Zoobook Series Created by
John Bonnett Wexo

Written by
Beth Wagner Brust

Zoological Consultant
Charles R. Schroeder, D.V.M.
Director Emeritus
San Diego Zoo &
San Diego Wild Animal Park

Scientific Consultants
Sam Ridgway, D.V.M., Ph.D.

Marianne Riedman, Ph.D.
Director, Sea Otter Research
Monterey Bay Aquarium

Creative Education

Art Credits

Illustrations by Tim Hayward. **Pages Eight and Nine: Main Art,** Walter Stuart; **Page Ten: Middle Left,** Walter Stuart; **Page Eleven: Upper Right,** Walter Stuart. **Activities Art:** Elizabeth Morales-Denney.

Photographic Credits

Front Cover: Kennan Ward (Kennan Ward Photography); **Pages Six and Seven:** Jeff Foott; **Page Eight:** M. Stouffer (Animals Animals); **Page Nine:** Gordon Menzie (Wildlife Education, Ltd.); **Page Twelve:** Gordon Menzie (Wildlife Education, Ltd.); **Page Thirteen: Top,** Jeff Foott (Bruce Coleman, Inc.); **Middle Left,** Alan Carey (Photo Researchers); **Lower Right,** Tom Bean (DRK Photo); **Pages Fourteen and Fifteen**: Jeff Foott; **Page Sixteen: Middle Left,** Art Wolfe (Allstock); **Lower Left,** S.J. Krasemann (Peter Arnold, Inc.); **Page Seventeen: Upper Right,** Jeff Foott (Tom Stack and Associates); **Lower Right,** Jeff Foott; **Page Nineteen: Upper Right,** Kathy Dawson (Dawson and Dawson); **Upper Left,** David Lissy (FPG International); **Lower Left,** Larry Ulrich (DRK Photo); **Pages Twenty and Twenty-one:** Frans Lanting (Minden Pictures); **Page Twenty-two: Upper Left,** Art Wolfe (Allstock); **Lower Left,** Gordon Menzie (Wildlife Education, Ltd.).

Our Thanks To: Anne Muraski (Friends of the Sea Otter); Dale Glantz (Kelco); Dr. O. Douglas Wilson (North Coast Pediatrics Medical Group); Linda Coates, Valerie Hare, Wendy Perkins (San Diego Zoo Library); Geoffrey Lowman; Enrique Newcomb; Erin Stuart; Sean Brust, Paul Brust.

Special Thanks To: Stan Lowe; Cynthia Wilson; T.R. Coleman, Larry Brass; Cheryl Gilman; Sal Tarrango; Bob Sheehan; Jacki Sporl, Bernard Thornton; Carmen Thulin; Bill Burch; Lois and Randolph Wood; Joe Selig.

Contents

Sea otters are truly irresistible. They are cute, cuddly-looking animals with friendly faces and playful personalities. It's hard to believe that these delightful creatures were once hunted almost to extinction. But at one time, sea otters were in great demand for their pelts to make fur coats. Fortunately, in recent years sea otters have made a remarkable comeback. And although some populations are still threatened, their numbers are increasing throughout most of their range.

Like the other 11 species of otters, sea otters belong to the weasel family. Like weasels, they are closely related to badgers, skunks, and minks. The scientific name for the sea otter is *Enhydra lutris*, which, not surprisingly, means "otter in the water."

This name fits sea otters well because they spend almost all of their time in the ocean — they eat, sleep, mate, give birth, and feed their young at sea. Sea otters are marine mammals. Like whales and other marine mammals, they breathe air. They feed milk to their young. They are warm-blooded. And they have hair on their bodies. But they are among the smallest of all marine mammals.

Found only in the North Pacific ocean, sea otters usually live along rocky shorelines where there are cliffs and sheltered coves. One hundred and fifty thousand sea otters live off of Alaska and the Soviet Union, while about 1,700 live along the coast of central California. Groups of sea otters, called *rafts*, can often be found among kelp beds where there is plenty of food.

Sea otters are playful by nature, and for this reason they are sometimes called the "clowns of the kelp bed." Another nickname for sea otters is "old men of the sea," because of the white whiskers they sometimes have on their faces.

In the following pages, you'll learn more about the wonderful sea otter. And you'll see why it is so important for us to do everything we can to save sea otters from any further threats of extinction.

Sea otters spend most of their time resting or swimming on their backs. They are the only marine mammals that eat, sleep, and carry their young while floating on their backs.

For its size, a sea otter's lungs are twice as large as those of other mammals. Large lungs give sea otters more oxygen for diving — and even help them float better.

When sea otters are in a hurry, they swim underwate on their stomachs. They pun their bodies up and down, pushing hard with their hi feet to move themselves forward.

A sea otter's body is even better adapted to life in the water than its cousin's, the river otter. That's because sea otters spend so much more time — almost all of it — in the water. And yet, sea otters are not as streamlined as seals, dolphins, and other marine mammals.

Sea otters are among the largest members of the otter family. Males grow to just over 4 feet long (1.2 meters), including the tail. And they weigh up to 100 pounds (45 kilograms), or about as much as a German shepherd. Female sea otters are a bit smaller, measuring just under 4 feet long and weighing up to 72 pounds (32.6 kilograms).

Powerful and graceful swimmers, sea otters have large muscles in their hindquarters to help them move forward in the water. And they have strong muscles in their forearms to help them pry off and pound open shellfish.

Sea otters can hear quite well, and they hold their small ears upright at the surface to listen for danger. But when diving, they point their ears downward to keep out the seawater.

Not all otters live in the ocean. In fact, all but two otter species live in fresh water. River otters, like the one at left, are smaller and less furry than sea otters. And they have longer legs so they can get around more easily on land.

When swimming in dark or murky water, sea otters use their sensitive whiskers to feel their way around and to find food. Whiskers also help sea otters feel vibrations in the water.

To get around at the surface, sea otters swim on their backs. Usually they kick their hind feet out to the sides. But sometimes they just swish their tails back and forth, without using their feet at all.

A sea otter's forepaws are very sensitive. Otters have claws—much like a cat's—that they can push out and pull in at will. They also have tough pads on their paws to help them grip slippery fish and pick up prickly sea urchins. Inside the paws, they have five individual fingers, much like your fingers.

If you look closely at a sea otter's hind foot, you will see that the *outside* toe is the longest and the *inside* toe is the smallest—just the opposite of your toes! But for otters, this makes sense. With a large outer toe, an otter can spread its hind feet wider for swimming.

See for yourself how a sea otter's paw works. Pull a sock over your hand. Now write with a pencil. See how well you can control the pencil, even though your thumb and fingers are covered. In the same way, a sea otter can manipulate objects, even though its paw is covered with a mitten-like skin.

Sea otters have strong jaw-bones and large, rounded teeth to help them crush the hard shells of clams, crabs, mussels, abalone, and sea urchins. Big lower teeth, called *incisors* (in-SIZE-urs), are used to scoop the meat out of the shells.

Sea otters have extremely flexible spines. This allows them to bend their bodies backward Ⓐ and forward Ⓑ in a complete circle. A flexible spine also enables a sea otter to reach every inch of its body when cleaning its fur. And as you'll find out on the next page, clean fur is very important to a sea otter.

Keeping their fur clean — or grooming — is a matter of life and death to sea otters. They are the only marine mammals that don't have a layer of fat, or blubber, to keep them warm in the cold ocean. Instead, they depend on their furry coats for warmth.

Sea otters have the *thickest* fur of any animal in the world. In fact, some otters have as many as a billion hairs on their bodies. But it's not the fur alone that keeps otters warm. Air bubbles trapped at the base of the fur also protect them from the ocean's chill.

Because their fur is so dense, sea otters must spend a great deal of time each day grooming themselves. If they don't groom, their fur gets matted and cannot hold air bubbles. Then the cold water can slip through to their bare skin, freezing the sea otter to death. By keeping clean, sea otters stay healthy and warm.

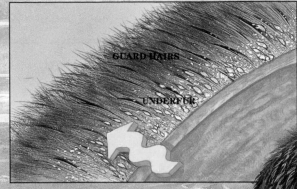

GUARD HAIRS

UNDERFUR

A sea otter has two types of fur. There are the long, coarse strands called *guard hairs*. And there are the shorter, finer hairs called *underfur*. When otters groom themselves, they are actually fluffing up their underfur to trap tiny air bubbles between each hair. These bubbles make a shield that blocks out the cold water.

①

See for yourself how air bubbles help a sea otter float. Fill a sink with water. Then push a dry sponge under the water. See all the bubbles coming out of the sponge as it fills with water. Now it barely floats. If a sea otter doesn't fluff up its fur often to trap bubbles, then it can't float as well either.

When a sea otter dives underwater, a constant stream of bubbles rises from its coat. Although these bubbles are essential for warmth, they may make it harder for an otter to get to the bottom to look for food.

②

Now squeeze out the wet sponge and set it on the water's surface. Notice how it floats higher in the water. That's because you've replaced the water with air bubbles. That's just what a sea otter does when it grooms itself, squeezing out the water to make room for the air bubbles.

A sea otter uses its forepaws as clamps to press water out of its fur. In addition to rubbing hard to get air next to its skin, an otter may blow into its thick coat. This traps even more air in the underfur.

Although a sea otter looks soft and cuddly, it would probably snap at anyone trying to pet its fur. Sea otters usually don't enjoy having their coats touched because this could soil their fur and even endanger them.

Using its sharp claws as a comb, a sea otter will scratch and brush its fur to untangle and clean it. A grooming sea otter will roll, twist, and squirm to reach every inch of its fur. Its coat is so loose on its body, an otter can pull it around to clean areas that are hard to reach.

Many dogs, like this German shepherd, also have thick fur — but it's not nearly as thick as sea otter fur. Otters have at least four times as much fur on their bodies as German shepherds do.

A German shepherd has only about 40,000 hairs per square inch, whereas a sea otter can have up to a million hairs per square inch! If you tried to part a dog's fur with a comb, you would be able to see the skin at the base of the fur.

DOG FUR

SEA OTTER FUR

Sea otter fur is so thick and dense, it would be impossible to part it with a comb and see the skin. Because sea otters need warm coats year-round, they don't shed all at once like other animals. Instead, they lose a few old hairs at a time — and grow a few new ones — all year long.

11

S ea otters eat many different types of food—and a lot of it! Shellfish is their favorite food, especially clams, scallops, mussels, and abalone. But they also like crabs, sea urchins, squid, snails, octopus, and fish. They prefer foods that they can pick up easily or pry off of rocks.

In areas where sea otters have been living for a long time, studies show that individual otters have their own favorite foods. Each otter eats only two or three types of foods. This could explain why so many otters can live peacefully in the same area.

To collect and eat their food, sea otters often use stones as tools. With the exception of humans and a few other primates, sea otters are the only mammals that use tools. They use stones as hammers to break loose abalone or mussels from the rocks. And they bang shellfish against stones to crack open their hard shells.

① To find food, a sea otter may dive 300 feet (91.4 meters). But otters usually prefer shallower water where food is easier to reach. Their average dive is 35 feet (10.6 meters) and lasts 1 to 2 minutes. But when necessary, a big otter can stay underwater for almost 4 minutes!

HEAT

HEAT

FOOD CHANGES INTO ENERGY

HEAT

Sea otters can change food into energy at a very fast rate. This energy heats up their bodies and keeps them warm. Even with their thick coats, sea otters lose body heat much faster than land animals do. So they need to eat a lot to keep their temperature up.

Sea otters eat one-quarter of their body weight in food *every day*. If you were like a sea otter, you would have to eat a mountain of food every day just to stay warm!

② When a sea otter finds shellfish or other foods, it stashes them in hidden pouches located under its forelegs. Then it returns to the surface to eat. A sea otter can carry as many as five small sea urchins at a time in each pouch.

Sea otters always float on their backs while eating. As soon as they've finished a meal, they roll over a few times to wash off bits of shell, food scraps, and fish slime. Rolling in the water also helps keep the food from getting stuck in their fur.

③ Once back at the surface, the sea otter prepares to eat. First, it balances a stone on its chest. Then, holding the food between both paws, it pounds the shell on the stone until it cracks open. The otter in this picture is about to eat a sea urchin.

People who harvest shellfish for a living blame sea otters for eating too many clams and abalone. It's true that otters do eat a lot of shellfish. But recent studies show that there are fewer shellfish all along the California coast—even in places where there are no sea otters! This suggests that it is *people* who are taking too many shellfish—not sea otters.

Kelp is the fastest-growing plant in the world. Kelp also provides homes for many types of sea creatures. Sea otters help kelp grow by eating its greatest enemy—sea urchins. Urchins devour kelp very quickly. With sea otters around, the urchin population is kept low so the kelp forests can grow well.

Kelp harvesting is a huge industry. Kelp tops are turned into a powder called alginate (AL-gen-AYTE), which is used as a thickener in milkshakes, ice cream, and toothpaste. It is also used in frozen dinners, juices, and salad dressings as well as in vitamins and medicines.

Alaskan sea otters

Few mothers are as loving and devoted to their young as sea otters. Sea otter pups need good mothers because they are totally helpless at birth. They can barely swim. They can't feed themselves. And they don't know how to clean their fur to stay warm.

For the first month of its life, a sea otter pup rests quietly on its mother's chest as she cuddles, grooms, and feeds it. Until the pup is about 6 months old, its mother never leaves it except to look for food. Sea otter mothers have only one pup at a time, probably because young pups need so much attention.

Generally, sea otters are social animals. Although they feed by themselves, they often gather together in rafts to rest in their favorite kelp bed. Sea otters are the only otters that group together this way.

Except for sharks, the bald eagle is a sea otter's only natural enemy. To feed its young, an eagle parent may swoop down and snatch a young pup from the water while its mother is off looking for food.

Sea otters spend as much time feeding at night as they do during the day—and so they nap for short periods whenever possible. Young or old, most sea otters sleep with their forepaws tucked under their chins or held over their eyes.

Sea otter pups are born on land and in the water. They weigh 4 to 5 pounds at birth (1.8 to 2.2 kilograms). Young pups, like the one you see here, spend most of their time resting on their mother's chest to stay warm and safe.

When a sea otter mother must leave her pup alone, she sometimes wraps it in kelp to keep it from drifting away on an ocean current. Even adult otters like to wrap themselves in kelp to sleep. But sea otters can sleep just as well floating on the open sea.

One of the very first things a sea otter pup needs to learn is how to groom its fur. And a good way for a pup to do this is by watching its mother. Pups must also learn how to dive, what foods to eat, and how to use a stone to crack open seashells.

Sea otter pups love to play and wrestle with each other. Sometimes they even play with their mothers or other adult otters. Such play is not only fun, but it also helps the pups develop important survival skills.

When escaping from danger, a sea otter mother tucks her pup under her foreleg and dives underwater. Or if the pup is large, she sinks her teeth into its loose fur and pulls it under. Pups are not strong enough to dive by themselves until they are 2 to 3 months old.

Mothers and pups — and other females — usually stay in rafts apart from the male otters. The largest raft of sea otters ever seen was in Alaska, and it had over 2,000 members. But most rafts are much smaller, with 50 to 100 otters. And in California, the average raft has only about a dozen animals.

People began hunting sea otters for their fur in the 1700s, and kept hunting them until 1911. The first people to bring otter furs to the marketplace were the Russians. They made so much money selling them that other nations began hunting otters, too. Close to 1 million sea otters died during this period. And the only reason the hunting stopped was that no more otters could be found. Although it seemed too late, a law was passed in 1911 making it illegal to hunt sea otters. This helped protect the few otters that remained.

Now there are new dangers to sea otters. The main threat is oil spills. Oil sticks to otters' fur and then they can't float or stay warm. Alaskan otters have already been injured by oil spills. And California otters are also at risk. To find out how you can help sea otters, write to Friends of the Sea Otter, P.O. Box 221220, Carmel, California 93922.

As the map shows, sea otters once lived all along the North Pacific coast (yellow areas). Today they can only be found along the Soviet Union, Alaska, and Central California (red areas).

People who hunted sea otters paddled their boats close to them and then killed them with guns or spears. Although native Alaskans had been hunting otters for years, it was not until foreigners began hunting them that their numbers declined.

When sea otters are alarmed or frightened, they hold their paws up in the air and hiss. If anyone comes too close, they dive under the water for safety.

Russians and other hunters took sea otter furs to traders. The traders then sold the furs to Asian and European markets. Furs were sold in London and other major cities to be made into coats, stoles, and other winter clothing.

Gill nets are used to catch fish, but sometimes sea otters and other marine mammals get tangled up in them, too. Under California law, fishermen cannot put their gill nets in water that is less than 120 feet deep (37 meters). A new law may push that limit to 180 feet (55 meters), which would make it even safer for sea otters.

Wherever people are boating too closely to sea otters, injuries can occur. Motorized jet skis are particularly dangerous for otters. Even though they have no propellor, jet skis can zip through kelp beds at top speeds — running over otters and sometimes injuring them seriously.

Oil prevents air bubbles from staying in an otter's fur. If rescued quickly, an oiled sea otter can be scrubbed with dish soap to clean its coat. But even if it is rescued, it can still get sick — especially if it swallowed any oil.

Off the coast of central California, a 100-mile-long sea otter refuge was established to protect otters from harm. But even outside of this refuge, sea otters are protected as a threatened species under national and state laws.

To increase their range and chances of survival, Alaskan sea otters have been moved to areas along the Pacific Northwest coast. Some of these relocated otters have begun new colonies.

California sea otters

SEA OTTERS ACTIVITIES

Try these otterly fun activities. Use what you have learned about sea otters to complete the exercises on these two pages.

Otter Dictionary

What's An Otter Word For... ?

Read each definition. Then write the otter word that it describes.
See back cover for answers

2. ■■■■: Sea plant

1. ■■■: Baby otter

3. ■■■: Keeps a sea otter warm

4. ■■■■: Body parts otters use to catch fish

5. ■■■■■: Flying otter predator

6. ■■■■■: Swimming otter predator

Answers:
1. Pup 2. Kelp 3. Fur 4. Paws 5. Eagles 6. Shark

There Otter Be A Law

Write letters to your senators and representatives asking them to support laws protecting otters and other animals. (You can find the names and addresses of lawmakers in the government pages of your phone book.)

Dear Senator,
Please pass laws to protect Sea Otters and other animals. I really care about them.
Sincerely,
Erin

In Otter Amazement

Help the mother sea otter find her way back to her pup. Don't let her get caught by any of the hazards. Along the way, help her find abalone, sea urchins, and clams to eat.

START

FINISH

You Otter Be In Pictures

Use the pictures below to help you answer these four questions about sea otters. *See back cover for answers.*

1. A group of sea otters.

2. Why sea otters are sometimes called "old men of the sea."

3. What sea otters help grow by eating sea urchins.

4. Three foods sea otters eat.

Answers:

Otterly Mathematical

A sea otter eats about 20% its body weight in food each day. To find out how much a 90-pound sea otter would eat, multiply the weight of the otter times 25%:

$90 \times .25 = 22.50$ pounds

How many pounds of food would *you* have to eat in one day to eat as much as a sea otter eats?

	x .25 =	
Your weight		Pounds of food per day

Index